Coolie Odyssey

David Dabydeen

HANSIB

This reprinted edition published in Great Britain in 2006
by Hansib Publications Limited
P.O. Box 226, Hertford, Hertfordshire SG14 3WY

Email: info@hansib-books.com
Website: www.hansib-books.com

First published in Great Britain in 1988
by Hansib Publications and Dangaroo Press

ISBN 1 870518 69 1

© David Dabydeen

Cover design by Graphic Resolutions, Hertfordshire, England

Design and Production by Books of Colour, Hertfordshire, England

Printed and bound in Great Britain

For Ma

(Amy Dabydeen, d. 1985)

Also by David Dabydeen

Hogarth, Walpole and Commercial Britain (Hansib, 1987)

A Reader's Guide to West Indian and Black British Literature
(Hansib, 1997) with Nana Wilson-Tagoe

India in the Caribbean (Hansib, 1987) ed., with Dr Brinsley Samaroo

Coolie Odyssey was originally published as part of Hansib's 'Coolie
Odyssey' series of books to mark the 150th anniversary – in
1988 – of the arrival of Indians in the Caribbean (1838-1988).

Other titles in the 'Coolie Odyssey' series

The Web of Tradition: Uses of Allusion in V.S. Naipaul's Fiction,
by John Thieme

India in the Caribbean, edited by Dr David Dabydeen and Dr
Brinsley Samaroo

Forbidden Freedom: The Story of British Guiana, by Cheddi Jagan

*Benevolent Neutrality: Indian Government Policy and Labour
Migration to British Guiana 1854-1884,* by Dr Basdeo Mangru

Indo-West Indian Cricket, by Frank Birbalsingh & Clem Shiwcharan

The Open Prison, by Angus Richmond

Inseparable Humanity: An Anthology of Reflections of Shridath Ramphal,
edited by Ron Sanders

King of the Carnival and other stories, by Willi Chen

4

Preface

The first poem started on a train journey from Edinburgh to Birmingham, with further pieces written in trains from Coventry to London and in planes from London over the Atlantic to the Caribbean. Lines came slowly, in fragments. The poems offer glimpses into an odyssey, not a chronicle of threaded events. The journey is from India to Guyana to England, and it is as much a journey of words as deeds. The encounter with whites, sketched in the early pieces, becomes more intense in the journey to England where the experiences are described in a series of poems about the 'White Woman' (Miranda/Britannia), taking up the central theme of my first book, *Slave Song*.

Poems

Poems

Coolie Odyssey

(For Ma, d. 1985)

Now that peasantry is in vogue,
Poetry bubbles from peat bogs,
People strain for the old folk's fatal gobs
Coughed up in grates North or North East
'Tween bouts o' living dialect,
It should be time to hymn your own wreck,
Your house the source of ancient song:
Dry coconut shells cackling in the fireside
Smoking up our children's eyes and lungs,
Plantains spitting oil from a clay pot,
Thick sugary black tea gulped down.

The calves hustle to suck,
Bawling on their rope but are beaten back
Until the cow is milked.
Frantic children call to be fed.
Roopram the Idiot goes to graze his father's goats backdam
Dreaming that the twig he chews so viciously in his mouth
Is not a twig.

In a winter of England's scorn
We huddle together memories, hoard them from
The opulence of our masters.

You were always back home, forever
As canefield and whiplash, unchanging
As the tombstones in the old Dutch plot
Which the boys used for wickets playing ball.

Over here Harilall who regularly dodged his duties at the
        marketstall
To spin bowl for us in the style of Ramadhin
And afterwards took his beatings from you heroically
In the style of England losing
Is now known as the local Paki
Doing slow trade in his Balham cornershop.
Is it because his heart is not in business
But in the tumble of wickets long ago
To the roar of wayward boys?
Or is it because he spends too much time
Being chirpy with his customers, greeting
The tight-wrapped pensioners stalking the snow
With tropical smile, jolly small chat, credit?
They like Harilall, these muted claws of Empire,
They feel privileged by his grinning service,
They hear steelband in his voice
And the freeness of the sea.
The sun beams from his teeth.

Heaped up beside you Old Dabydeen
Who on Albion Estate clean dawn
Washed obsessively by the canal bank,
Spread flowers on the snake-infested water,
Fed the gods the food that Chandra cooked,
Bathed his tongue of the creole
Babbled by low-caste infected coolies.
His Hindi chants terrorized the watertoads
Flopping to the protection of bush.
He called upon Lord Krishna to preserve
The virginity of his daughters
From the Negroes,
Prayed that the white man would honour
The end-of-season bonus to Poonai
The canecutter, his strong, only son:
Chandra's womb being cursed by deities

Like the blasted land
Unconquerable jungle or weed
That dragged the might of years from a man.
Chandra like a deaf-mute moved about the house
To his command,
A fearful bride barely come-of-age
Year upon year swelling with female child.
Guilt clenched her mouth
Smothered the cry of bursting apart:
Wrapped hurriedly in a bundle of midwife's cloth
The burden was removed to her mother's safekeeping.
He stamped and cursed and beat until he turned old
With the labour of chopping tree, minding cow, building fence
And the expense of his daughters' dowries.
Dreaming of India
He drank rum
Till he dropped dead
And was buried to the singing of Scottish Presbyterian hymns
And a hell-fire sermon from a pop-eyed bawling catechist,
By Poonai, lately baptised, like half the village.

Ever so old,
Dabydeen's wife,
Hobbling her way to fowl-pen,
Cussing low, chewing her cud, and lapsed in dream,
Sprinkling rice from her shrivelled hand.
Ever so old and bountiful,
Past where Dabydeen lazed in his mudgrave,
Idle as usual in the sun,
Who would dip his hand in a bowl of dhall and rice –
Nasty man, squelching and swallowing like a low-caste sow –
The bitch dead now!

The first boat chugged to the muddy port
Of King George's Town. Coolies come to rest
In El Dorado,

Their faces and best saris black with soot.
The men smelt of saltwater mixed with rum.
The odyssey was plank between river and land,
Mere yards but months of plotting
In the packed bowel of a white man's boat
The years of promise, years of expanse.
At first the gleam of the green land and the white folk and
      the Negroes,
The earth streaked with colour like a toucan's beak,
Kiskidees flame across a fortunate sky,
Canefields ripening in the sun
Wait to be gathered in armfuls of gold.

I have come back late and missed the funeral.
You will understand the connections were difficult.
Three airplanes boarded and many changes
Of machines and landscapes like reincarnations
To bring me to this library of graves,
This small clearing of scrubland.
There are no headstones, epitaphs, dates.
The ancestors curl and dry to scrolls of parchment.
They lie like texts
Waiting to be written by the children
For whom they hacked and ploughed and saved
To send to faraway schools.
Is foolishness fill your head.
Me dead.
Dog-bone and dry-well
Got no story to tell.
Just how me born stupid is so me gone.
Still we persist before the grave
Seeking fables.
We plunder for the maps of El Dorado
To make bountiful our minds in an England
Starved of gold.

Albion village sleeps, hacked
Out between bush and spiteful lip of river.
Folk that know bone
Fatten themselves on dreams
For the survival of days.
Mosquitoes sing at a nipple of blood.
A green-eyed moon watches
The rheumatic agony of houses crutched up on stilts
Pecked about by huge beaks of wind,
That bear the scars of ancient storms.
Crappeau clear their throats in hideous serenade,
Candleflies burst into suicidal flame.
In a green night with promise of rain
You die.

We mark your memory in songs
Fleshed in the emptiness of folk,
Poems that scrape bowl and bone
In English basements far from home,
Or confess the lust of beasts
In rare conceits
To congregations of the educated
Sipping wine, attentive between courses –
See the applause fluttering from their white hands
Like so many messy table napkins.

The Old Map

Empty treasure chests dumped from departed ships
And jettisoned slaves washed
Into an arc from Jamaica to Guiana.
Islands aborted from the belly of sea
Forever unborn in rock and swamp.
Other fragments rot in the sun
Like cane chewed and spat
From coolie mouth.
Haiti is a crab with broken claw.
Cuba droops in fear at the foot of America.
Blue is deep and everywhere of European eye,
Green of seamen's hope and gangrene,
Yellow of the palm of dead Amerindian
Unyielding gold.

El Dorado

Juncha slowly dying of jaundice
Or yellow fever or blight or jumbie or neighbour's spite,
No-one knows why he turns the colour of cane.

Small boys come to peep, wondering
At the hush of the death-hut
Until their mothers bawl them out.

Skin flaking like goldleaf
Casts a halo round his bed.
He goes out in a puff of gold dust.

Bathed like a newborn child by the women.
Laid out in his hammock in the yard.
Put out to feel the last sun.

They bury him like treasure,
The coolie who worked two shillings all day
But kept his value from the overseer.

Coolie Mother

Jasmattie live in bruk –
Down hut big like Bata shoe-box,
Beat clothes, weed yard, chop wood, feed fowl
For this body and that body and every blasted body,
Fetch water, all day fetch water like if the whole –
Whole slow-flowing Canje river God create
Just for *she* one own bucket.

Till she foot-bottom crack and she hand cut-up
And curse swarm from she mouth like red-ants
And she cough blood on the ground but mash it in:
Because Jasmattie heart hard, she mind set hard

To hustle save she one-one slow penny,
Because one-one dutty make dam cross the Canje
And she son Harilall *got* to go school in Georgetown,
Must wear clean starch pants, or they go laugh at he,
Strap leather on he foot, and he *must* read book,
Learn talk proper, take exam, go to England university,
Not turn out like he rum-sucker chamar dadee.

* *dutty*: piece of earth
* *chamar*: low-caste

18

Coolie Son

(The toilet attendant writes home)

Taana boy, how you do?
How Shanti stay? And Sukhoo?
Mosquito still a-bite all-you?
Juncha dead true-true?
Mala bruk-foot set?
Food deh foh eat yet?

Englan nice, snow and dem ting,
A land dey say fit for a king,
Iceapple plenty on de tree and bird a-sing –
Is de beginning of what dey call 'The Spring'.

And I eating enough for all a-we
And reading book bad-bad.

But is what make Matam wife fall sick
And Sonnel cow suck dry wid tick?

Soon, I go turn lawya or dacta,
But, just now, passage money run out
So I tek lil wuk –
I is a Deputy Sanitary Inspecta,
Big-big office, boy! Tie round me neck!
Brand new uniform, one big bunch keys!
If Ma can see me now how she go please....

Missie and the Coconut Man

Toolsie's task:
Coconut gripped in outstretched hand
Ready to pelt like cricket ball,
Two twitches of his cutlass, preparatory,
Batsman tapping at the crease,
Then downward swoop of blade
Hard, straight, unequivocal –
And head chop clean off,
Boss bowler blasting away the bail.

Or spinning the thing in his palm
Chipping here and there
Shaving and shaping a pleasing mouth,
Cutlass crafting victory,
The cunning of a coolie Ramadhin:

Whilst Missie waits indifferent to the fantasy
Fingering her riding whip impatiently.

* *Ramadhin*: Legendary Indo-Caribbean bowler of googlies

Day's End

'They gone far Toolsie!
In the darkness of dancehall
Sita shaking she hip and Negro shaking back,
Loud noise, lipstick and loose brassières,
How these children got no shame, and hard-ears.
The girl fretting whenever I mention marriage:
Poonai's son is nice quiet boy and got job on shopfloor,
But coolie not for her no more,
They gone too far Toolsie!'

One long wife-wailing and a hollering –

Like when magistrate jail cow-thief
Or dog-fuck when they struggling to leggo,
Like when Ramlall Ma hear he fail exam
After she toiling nightshift with Overseer to buy schoolbook,
Or when someone burn down Chinee shop
Since he stop give credit by summonsing folk instead –

Toolsie endures, dreaming of bat-and-ball
In backyard with the village boys,
From the haze of his evening hammock and rum-bottle,
Cane splinters still jammed in his foot from the day's work.

The Untouchable

Juncha dream big.
Too lazy to work penny a day
Like the rest of we:
Is white woman he see.
Eye swell with botheration ever since he
Peep in white man parlour and stare hungry-belly
At sofa, chandelier, chinaware, and picture of Jesus
Saying ALL WILL BE GIVEN TO YE WHO TRUST IN ME,
And spread out on veranda, Missie,
Flowing like milk-froth in her loose white frock –
Now everytime Juncha squeeze cow bubby
He imagine her skin how it smooth and cream
How her ankle small and pretty like calf-foot
And the sun dripping gold in her hair –
Ever since Juncha a-chop careless in canefield
Muttering to himself like man a-talk in dream –

Juncha, let her be!
You born for poverty, you is coolie!
The woman not make for you and me!
And if white man catch you, is heng you heng from tree!

But you think Juncha listening to we?
The man deaf to insult or the threat of injury.
Sometimes he gathering cane up like a bundle of love
Resting it gently in the punt like bridal bed,
Gazing upon it gleaming in the sunshine,
Or else the man dark with passion like raincloud
Drifting lonely in the blueness of her eye

Ready to burst upon her white body –
Is mad he mad with some deep pain or mystery.

Juncha, let her be!
You born for misery, you is mattie!
The woman not make for you and me!
And if white man catch you, whip go wake you battie!

* *mattie*: shipmate (cargo of coolies)
* *battie*: backside

For Rohan Bholalall Kanhai

1.

Kanhai
Cutlass whack six,
Leather-ball red
Like Whiteman restless eye.
One ton cane-runs
Cropped, all day in hot sun the man cut
And drop on he back
To hook two and lash four:
Hear the coolies crying out for more!
England glad bad when clouds
Puff and scowl and blue
Like end-of-over-bowlerman
And day done in rainburst:
God is White Overseer for true!

2.

And when darkness break and Blackman buss we head
Wismar-side and bleed up we women
And Burnham blow down we house and pen
Like fireball and hurricane
And riverboat pack with crying and dead
Like Old Days come back of lash and chain,
Is round night radio we huddle to catch news
Of Kanhai batting lonely in some far country
Call Warwick-Shire, and every ball blast
Is cuff he cuffing back for we,

Driving sorrow to the boundary,
Every block-stroke is paling in a fence
He putting down to guard we,
And when century come up, is like dawn!

* *Wismar*. Scene of massacre of Indians in Guyana by Africans, in the 1960s.
* *Burnham*, later President of the country, was a promoter of racial strife.

Christmas in the Caribbean

Sky raining cane-ash plant-scab black miracle.
Big bellied women bawl bloodcloth
Run salvage wardrobe from washline.

Slow sore-footed children mincing along rock road,
Sun blazing down, jungle haze, coolie boy scream,
Waspmouth ripe, bite, snake strike by waterpipe.

These shrivelled wise ones burn weed, chant, dance, and pray
Envisioned, whilst rat gnaw straw, yardfowl peck-peck
At fat cockroach.

Cutlass swing sing to cane in mystic trance:
Wuk! bruk! suck! muck! fuck!
But cane is we stubborn Cross, it don't give one scunt for
        Romance.

The secret is not to born or get dead quick,
Stone, nail, drown the puppies, the babies,
Cannibalize she nipple, mother-cord, devour she disease.

Burning down the Fields

1.

In moonless nights you make cane-ash weep
Over the land, blackening
The tooth of the overseer, twitching
His hand with dream of revenge.

Three or four small-boned coolies
Swifter than snake, weaving
Through cane, wakened
To faintest noise or ghostly light.

A hand is guided to the root
By the grace of candleflies.
You sprinkle oil in wordless ceremony,
You feed your spirits to the earth.

Night faints in the kerosene fumes.
You scratch a match to its heart and await
Exploding drum-beat, mash –
Ing-down-the-road feet
Of creole carnival.

2.

Windrushed the flames reach the shores of England,
Chars, chamars disembarking from boat-trains.
They will encrust the Shiny Monuments,
They will besmirch the White Page with their own words,
They will cremate their relatives on the Riverbank

And the Tiber will foam with halal-blood
And the Maidens will faint, or bear bastards
If the Lion lies down with the woolly-headed beast.

3.

i am not built for work
like bus-conducting
or lifting factory box
i want to get on in this world
as soon as i save some cash
i will open up a corner-shop –
then you won't see me for dust
i will make the children burn
electricity late at night reading
book that will take them to university
and give them bright certificate.

4.

This summer's day black people beat with life,
Waking to sun-blast, reggae-birdsong,
Youth preen their bodies, put on their disco robes:
The police will make music with their sirens
And the home-owners will play their burglar alarms
And dance will grip the heels of the crucified
And the wood-chips on the black people's shoulders
Will heap up huge bonfires around which
The wretched will gather to give praise
To the overpowering love of God
Who will not forsake the aim of his people
But will guide the stone to thinnest point of glass,
Bank, Bingo Hall, Jobcentre, and a Bookshop
Selling slim volumes of English verse.

* In 1948 the *Empire Windrush* docked at Tilbury bearing 492 Jamaicans, the
first boatload of post-war immigrants.

London Taxi Driver

From Tooting, where I picked him up, to Waterloo,
He honked, swerved, swore,
Paused at the twin-tubbed buttocks of High Street Wives,
Jerked forward again,
Unwound the window as we sped along,
Hawked and spat.

The talk was mostly solitary,
Of the new single, of missing the pools by bleeding two,
Of some sweet bitch in some soap serial,
How he'd like to mount and stuff her lipsticked mouth,
His eyes suddenly dreamy with designs –
Nearly missing a light he slammed the car stop,
Snatched the hand-brake up.
Wheel throbbed in hand, engine giddy with anticipation.
As we toured the slums of Lambeth the meter ticked greedily.

He has come far and paid much for the journey
From some village in Berbice where mule carts laze
And stumble over broken paths,
Past the women with buckets on their heads puffed
With ghee and pregnancy,
Past the men slowly bent over earth, shovelling,
Past the clutch of mud huts jostling for the shade,
Their Hindu flags of folk defiant rituals
That provoked the Imperial swords of Christendom
Discoloured, hang their heads and rot
On bamboo pikes:
Now he knows more the drama of amber red and green,

Mutinies against double-yellow lines,
His aggression is horned like ancient clarions,
He grunts rebellion
In back seat discount sex
With the night's last whore.

The New Poetry

She wanted to be alone with her world, vexed
Always by his prehistoric eye,
The strange usurping tales of anthropophagi
And recitation of colonial texts.

Britannia is serviced by new machines
Humming and twinkling as they work,
The creak of mule-drawn punt or old slave feet,
The exhalation of the aborigines

Are esoteric notes in a scholar's curious book:
The new poetry quietly observes
The ways a leaf spirals neutrally to earth,
The shades of moon, the tides, the shepherd's timeless crook.

She forsook as tedious his confession,
His alien unbridgeable babble of words,
Settling comfortably on the sofa
She would turn the television on

And see confirmed the greetings beamed through space
Of natives singing by some runway,
The bone-shaped plane of fat white men and foreign aid
Met by loud spears and women jigging waist.

Impotence

He waits below you
Like a deep earth hole
That snakes and eyeless insects make
Through shame of revelation.
The blue moon-motherness of your eye
Watches over broken adolescence
Suffocating in its tight black skin.

Swollen with gold
The imperial cane
Stampedes the land
Sun-god and overseer
To whom he pays
Tribute of his mother.

Now, in the blueness of your gaze
He dreams
The interminable sea,
Strapped horizontal to the deck,
The interminable sky,
Now, in the glow and gentle touch of your hair
He dreams
The stiff pike of cane
The failed insurrection.

The Seduction

(For Catherine Jane)

She said her name was Kate
And whether he would mate
On such and such a date
Or else tonight before too late
Before the pause to contemplate
Before the history and the hate.

> I cannot come to you tonight
> With monstrous organ of delight
> I have no claw no appetite
> I am not Caliban but sprite
> But weakness flutterance and flight
> An insect scurrying from the light.

She said her name was really Jane
That she was sweet as sugarcane
Unblighted by colonial reign
That all he wanted was some pain
To wrap himself in mythic chain
And labour in his self-disdain.

> You know that I am flaccid black
> Yet stretch my skin upon a rack
> That I may reach whereof I lack
> And scrape away the mange and plaque
> Of legacy and looking back
> Obliterate the ancient track

That I am naked lost in shame
Without the fantasy and game
The rules that history did proclaim –
I am the torture: you the flame
I am the victim: you the blame –
Tell me again, what is your name?

> Britannia it is not she cries!
> Miranda also she denies!
> Nor map nor piracy nor prize
> Nor El Dorado in disguise
> With pity gazed into his eyes
> And saw he could not improvise

So left him to his impotence
Imperial madness and pretence
The razor of historic sense
Of conquests bloody and immense
To which he offered no defence
But whimpered, bled in deference.

The Sexual Word

She dreaded the naivety
Of longing for rebirth,
Beheld him stuttering out his dream
Of journeys ended:
The howling oceanic thrust of history
That heaved forth savages in strange canoes
Weighed with magical cannon and muzzle and anklechain,
Stilled
To a pool in his eye
Through which he saw
The solitary quay
The new seed.

He burnt his mind in acid of his own alchemy
Urging song from his hurt mouth
Desperate to colonize her
In images of gold and fertility
To remake her from his famished rib
To redeem her from the white world
That would reduce him to mute captivity.

She refused the embrace of fantasy,
Unable to be torn up, transplanted,
Stripped, raped, broken and made to bear
Beautiful bastard fruit –
She could not endure the repetition
Necessary for new beginning

Yet was ravished by the poetry.

Miranda

His black bony peasant body
Stalk of blighted cane
In dry earth.

I will blot out the tyrant sun
Cleanse you in the raincloud of my body
In the secrecy of night set you supple and erect.

And wiped him with the moist cloth of her tongue
Like a new mother licking clean its calf
And hugged milk from her breast to his cracked mouth.

That when he woke he cried to dream again
Of the scent of her maternity
The dream of the moon of her deep spacious eye

Sea-blue and bountiful
Beyond supplication or conquest
A frail slave vessel wracked upon a mere pebble of her
            promise.

And the sun resumed its cruelty
And the sun shook with imperial glee
At the fantasy.

Caliban

The first night
I endured your creation
We talked desperately
Foraging the details of my youth
Like two tramps at a tip:
Finding riches among the rubble was your Romance.
I remember diving into the pit but coming up
Glittering in your eye –
Goldleaf or edge of assegai:
You were always bountiful with fantasy,
Fashioning me your Image or casting me Native:
White woman, womb of myth, foundry or funeral pyre
Where like a Hindu corpse I burn and shrink
To be reborn to your desire!

Afterwards, when the drunkenness of words
Receded, the pool of myth
Evaporated to uncomfortable sweat,
The residue of memory
Of a mere instant of delight,
You, in the cruelty of morning flight,
Face composed and underclothing
Unruffled by experience,
Return so crisply, so unambiguously
To sunlight.

Whilst I, coiled blackly within myself,
Paralysed with rage and wonder,
Straining still to sense your presence,
Craving still the magic of your making.

Rebel Love

When first he put his black hand to her breast, waiting
The whiplash, white man bellowing pain,
Pigs with bruised testicles battering their pen,
He dreamt a cornucopia of slaves poured overboard,
The suck of sharks, bleached, boned,
Washed up in Berbice,
He dreamt the dance of flames on coolieman skin
Running amok, screamed, smouldered to ash
To fertilize the canefields of Demerara,
He dreamt the dogs unloosed howling through the bush
Where, drunk with disobedience, stumbling,
Abandoned to her flesh,
He fell and lay
Still.

Water With Berries

A long night of instant love
In which he spent her sense of pain
Lapped at her ego
Like the mouth of beasts
Met in darkness at water's edge,
A long night of adoration
Lubrication, murmurings,
In which he fleshed her frame of waste
Sucked her distress
Like berries from her gaping vein,
That she was light-headed, bedded,
And fresh again with laughter:
So afterwards she confessed it
Taking the home train to Cheltenham
From his basement in Balham
Never again wanting to meet:
The English are so effortlessly complete.
Whilst he, forever imprisoned
In a romance of history
Emerges from sleep as from ship's bowel
Desperate to dream again
In her white spacious body
Fresh burning air
Blinding light
Song of bursting chain.

New World Words

She wanted to suck words,
Violate some mystery,
Feed deep, delirious
Into some gleaming tropical vein,
Sharp-beaked hummingbird
Drunk on the sweat of jungle flower.

He clamped his loins
From her consumptive mouth
Burning with shame
Of the cry of whiplashed coolie
Curled away shyly
To a finger of feeble ash.

And his speech was plain and impotent
As English drizzle on gritty pavement-stone,
No strange, lingering, soulful fiction
Of forest flute
Nor bark of trapped beast,
The darkness of his skin enfolded
No bewitchment.

Whilst she, in the dull plumage
Of her elderly civilization,
Empty, expressionless,
Fat with boredom, familiar, sluggish
Like a London pigeon in a dreary London street,
Longing to be startled into primeval flight,
Longing for the giddiness of hummingbird
Sipping at brilliant flower.

Wanting to be Born

(A Christmas poem)

you are fun girl white flesh ebullience
dizzy scents diamond garlanded bright desires
crystal-sharp gift-wrapped laughter dancing
in glitter of showcase abundance of
magical machines belong to you
speed your inheritance
style luxuriance

He cries of the wound of your wealth
His mind big with ambition
The belly of an Ethiopian.
He eats shimmering dry sand
Mirage of your flowing breast.

He plants a bone in your heart
Awaiting nurture and blossom.
He bears as Magus-tribute
A crutch and pedestal for your conscience.
The hunger of his ribs reveal,
Like the spokes of stars,
The wisdom of the slow dying world.

you are carolling christmas tree streamers merrily
ripples gilded icing-sweet jingling
bells of silver coin despise
his suckling mouth
the expectation of his seed

Christmas in England

(For Jane turned Third World journalist)

Daylight eclipses self-disdain.
Crushed flesh in a crowded morning train
Aborts the deeper pain.

Typewriters score and orchestrate
The human grunt. You recreate
Truth in journalistic prose,
Rearrange innocence in photographic pose.

The world partitioned in bylines
By the new imperial Pharisees. Headlines
Herald new markets, and wise men follow signs.

An organ blares, a congregation sings,
A corpse arises and sprouts angel-wings,
A widow breaks down before bread and wine:
She will take a holiday in the sunshine,
She will write thank you cards and place an ad,
She will read his obituary and be sad.

Then evening film or discothèque,
Jewels worn upon your neck
Like beacons to foretell a wreck.
Afterwards you fall asleep
In someone's snore and keep.

Daylight darkens the memory
Of a dream of poverty.
In the illumination of shops and offices

You are haloed from restlessness,
Strolling to the station of Charing Cross,
Reading the news on the bus to Shepherd's Bush.

Ma Talking Words

You only fool yourself when you say
The woman shallow as the water
She cleanse she make-up in
And you out of your precious depth.
Fact is the world want she
And all you can do is curse cut throat and despair
Or more crazy still
Write poetry:
That is dream and air!
You can't make pickni from word
Howsoever beautiful or raging:
The world don't know word.

Next time you lay down with she
And the white flesh wrench and bite like ratmouth
And she moaning fill you with pride,
But after you feel suck dry, throw-away like eggshell or seed,
Think that all-body here know your heart still flesh with good
And this village ground never grow more bright boy before
Who move out from mud and walk England
And we who stay back
Mash-mouth and crack
Still feed in you.

And how she go understand all that burden and fruit
You bear for we?
And how she go crave your soul and seed
Who always eat plenty
From different pot?
Book learning you got,

But history done dead, hard like teeth and bone
And white people don't want heal their own scar or hear their
        own story
And you can't hug them with bruk hand
Or lash sense in them with overseer stick.

Young and fresh and pretty
She swallow the world and get belly,
Rub lipstick on she mouth and make joke,
Nightlong music shake she foot.
All man a-take from she and go their way
Whilst stupid you want stay
Pan love like diamond from dirt
And dream that the world know word.

On Her Unfaithfulness

They were not accustomed to space
Except a piece of porthole showing sky
Imagined, or shovelled into logies,
Doorways cracked open to canefields choked with work.
His mother dropped a new child every year
And all affection was crowded out.
His mother was a sackful of crabs in her womb, scratching
Up, mashing
Up, clawing
For air.
Now you must surely see
Why he seeks
The wide space and sole portion of your heart
In which to be singularly free.

And all my furious talk of fidelity
Was because of that you see.

* *logies*: Old slave barracks which housed newly arrived indentured labourers

Homecoming

Only think you'll soon drop,
Stop sell pavement mango sun-beat –
Ing-day-long, with all the things you dreamed
To taste in the tourists' bags,
How they clearly passing you by like beggarman
But perplexed your blessed sunshine country
Should breed such you-lice, shacks.

Especially the long-legged bejewelled women boldly
Going where roach with sense would hesitate
In search of genuine native crafts
In poor people's shops
By uncharted alleys.

I brace you up against a wall
Doom-laden, mugging you for a life-story.
I trade you rum for old-time Indian talk
But you stutter creole stupidness, yielding
No gift but a sackful of green mangoes.

History we greed for in England,
Must know coolie ship, whip, brown paddy-skins
Burst, blown far by winds,
Whilst pearl-white rice feed overseer-mouth:
England, where it snows but we still born brown,
That I come back from to here, home,
As hungry as any white man for native gold,
To plant flag and to map your mind.

Catching Crabs

Ruby and me stalking savannah
Crab season with cutlass and sack like big folk.
Hiding behind stones or clumps of bush
Crabs locked knee-deep in mud mating
And Ruby seven years old feeling strange at the sex
And me horrified to pick them up
Plunge them into the darkness of bag,
So all day we scout to catch the lonesome ones
Who don't mind cooking because they got no prospect
Of family, and squelching through the mud,
Cutlass clearing bush at our feet,
We come home tired slow, weighed down with plenty
Which Ma throw live into boiling pot piece-piece.
Tonight we'll have one big happy curry feed,
We'll test out who teeth and jaw strongest
Who will grow up to be the biggest
Or who will make most terrible cannibal.

We leave behind a mess of bones and shell
And come to England and America
Where Ruby hustles in a New York tenement
And me writing poetry at Cambridge,
Death long catch Ma, the house boarded up
Breeding wasps, woodlice in its dark-sack belly:
I am afraid to walk through weed yard,
Reach the door, prise open, look,
In case the pot still bubbles magical
On the fireside, and I see Ma
Working a ladle, slow –

Limbed, crustacean-old, alone,
In case the woodsmoke and curry steam
Burn my child-eye and make it cry.

Post-Independence

(On the assassination of Dr Walter Rodney in 1980, in Guyana. Rodney, poking fun at President Sampson Burnham's delusions of Kingship, had publicly baptised him 'King Kong'.)

And from his mountain view the mighty Warrior
Beat upon his hirsute breast the messages of Government
That echoed through the foliage of coconut, banana –
His name was Sam Baboona and he was big Bwana.

Bursting and leaping and swinging they came to his
charismatic call
Whooping through the valleys in numbers that appal.

"I AM", he uttered, slowly glancing round,
Gathering the saliva supremely in his mouth,
"ME, ME BIG MASSA, ME IS KING
FROM HEAD TO TOE FROM HAND TO MOUTH
         FROM BACK TO FRONT,
AND ALL AYUH RASS AND ALL AYUH SCUNT!"
With that he paused, and spat, and sucked his teeth,
And pricked his ears, and picked his nose, as was his wont.

Such the majesty of man, such elegance, élan.
They stomped and shrieked and cheered and to their weapons
         ran.
The Warrior gave the sacred sign, the virgin bled, the hunt
         began.

Tarzan hurries to the scene, their folly to repair,
Alas, too late, as Rodney stumbles to the spear.

New Day Children

akbar akbar

ba$ll^{oOn}i_ng$ heavenwards to his creator
wheeeee! there he blows!

sita makes folk tune
when the wind flies
through her flute-bones

jessica's stomach is a spinning-top
her head a shiny spindle
round and round she dances in a faint

caesar contracts or bloats
like an accordion
presses or releases the button on his belly

rajah stretched
over ribs like drumskin
bangs his enamel bowl against stone

is massa day done! carnival come!
and all the children performing on Independence stage
fine, like flags unfurled in wind

Dependence, or the Ballad of the Little Black Boy

(On Francis Wheatley's 'Family Group and Negro Boy' painted in the 1770s)

Painterman come one day to our house
Whilst Missie try out her expensive blouse
And Massa make me cut his toenail
And muse aloud how nigger like snail
I rush fetch his trousers shoe and hair brush
And the padding to put in place of his crotch.

Missie cry out loud and tear off her dress
Put on another and curse in distress
Poor Ebony running from wardrobe to bed
Where Missie collapse as if truly dead
And Ebony dreaming the bitch gone to hell
When Missie wake her with one mighty yell.

Henry and James two right little dears
Who play with each other under the stairs
Who threaten if I tell to whip my behind
Or else squeeze my hand all gentle and kind
And give me their sweets their crayons and toys
Whisper darkly in my ears 'Boys will be boys'.

Lastly Miss Harriet and her pet dog
Whom she takes to her bed and takes to her bog
Serves him choicest meat on rich china plate –
Never mind the beggars waiting at the gate –
In my next life God please don't make me black
I want to be an English dog when I come back.

The two lovely boys and Massa, Missie
Herodotus (the dog) Miss Harriet and me

All gathered in the garden underneath a tree
They move me here, there, then finally agree
That whole day long I must stoop on one knee
And all the time I'm dying for a pee.

Whilst painterman splash, drip, dip, rearrange
And produce picture marvellously strange
How fair they seem and full of grace
Benevolence and love spread upon each face
And me at the edge typical of my race
Holding back the urine the hurt and disgrace.